George H Pettis

Kit Carson's Fight with the Comanche and Kiowa Indians,

at the Adobe Walls on the Canadian River, November 25th, 1864

George H Pettis

Kit Carson's Fight with the Comanche and Kiowa Indians,
at the Adobe Walls on the Canadian River, November 25th, 1864

ISBN/EAN: 9783744790260

Printed in Europe, USA, Canada, Australia, Japan

Cover: Foto ©ninafisch / pixelio.de

More available books at **www.hansebooks.com**

KIT CARSON'S FIGHT

WITH THE

COMANCHE AND KIOWA INDIANS,

AT THE ADOBE WALLS, ON THE CANADIAN RIVER,

NOVEMBER 25TH, 1864.

BY GEORGE H. PETTIS,

(Brevet Captain U. S. Volunteers, late First Lieutenant First Infantry, California Volunteers, and
Lieutenant and Adjutant First Infantry, New Mexico Volunteers.)

———◆———

PROVIDENCE:
SIDNEY S. RIDER.
1878.

= 83

.863

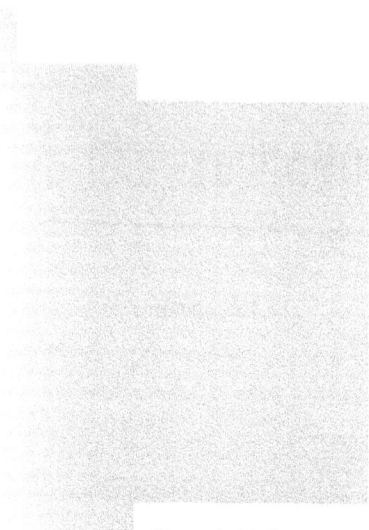

KIT CARSON'S FIGHT

WITH THE

COMANCHE AND KIOWA INDIANS.

———◆———

THE summer of 1864 will long be remembered by
our frontiersmen as a season when the Comanche, the
Kiowa, the Arapahoe, the Cheyenne, and the Plain
Apache held high carnival on our western plains.
From the early spring of that year, when the hardy
Indian pony could subsist on the growing grass of
the prairies, until late in the fall, they committed
their depredations, and there was not a week of that
whole season, but that some outrage was committed
by them. They seemed to have conceived the idea
that the white man could be exterminated, and by
concerted action, and by striking at different points,
to have fondly hoped that they could once more
roam and hunt at their pleasure, free and unmolested

by the white man's civilization. The determined
operations of the western Indians and their concerted action at this time, has led some to believe
that it was a part of the programme of, and that
they had been incited to this by, the leaders of the
rebellion. It seems plausible, too, for when the
grand old Army of the Potomac was fighting the battles of the Wilderness, of Spottsylvania, of North
Anna, of Cold Harbor, and Petersburg, and the
Weldon Railroad, Ream's Station, Peeble's Farm,
and Boydtown Road; and Sheridan had rode his
"twenty miles from Winchester town," and had
driven Early out of the Shenandoah valley; and
Sherman was fighting the battles that led to the capture of Atlanta, the Indians were spreading havoc
and destruction in all directions. No trains crossed
the plains that season without being attacked, and
none but those with strong military escorts escaped
capture and destruction. Houses and barns on the
frontier were fired, stock of all kinds was nowhere
secure, large and small parties were attacked, men,
women, and children murdered. In fact, the year
1864 will be sadly remembered as long as the pres-

ent generation of frontiersmen lives. The commanders of the different military departments bordering on this territory, had, with the few men at their command, sent out during the summer several expeditions, as escorts to trains, but they had accomplished no more than to accord safety to their different charges, as the mode of Indian warfare is to only give battle when they have all of the advantages.*

In the month of October, 1864, General James H. Carleton, then commanding the Department of New Mexico, believing that the Comanches and Kiowas might be found, on the south side of the Canadian river, in winter quarters, issued a general order, directing an expedition against these Indians. The command was ordered to consist as follows: Colonel Christopher Carson, (familiarly known as "Kit Carson,") First New Mexico Cavalry, commanding; Colonel Francisco P. Abreú, First New Mexico In-

* At the reading of this paper, before the Soldiers and Sailors Historical Society, February 14th, 1877, a gentleman who had visited the Indian Territory immediately at the   ared me that the supposition that the   e Indians to commit their atrocities   ing been so informed by several of th

fantry; Major William McCleave, First California
Cavalry; Captain Emil Fritz, Company B, First
California Cavalry, one officer and forty enlisted
men; Lieutenant Sullivan Heath, Company K, First
California Cavalry, one officer and forty men; Cap-
tain Merriam, Company M, First California Cavalry,
one officer and thirty-four men; Lieutenant George
H. Pettis, Company K, First California Infantry,
one officer and twenty-six men, with two twelve
pounder mountain howitzers mounted on prairie carriages; Captain Charles Deus, Company M, First
New Mexico Cavalry, two officers and seventy men;
Captain Joseph Berney, Company D, First New
Mexico Cavalry, two officers and thirty-six men;
Company A, First California Veteran Infantry, seventy-five men; Assistant Surgeon George S. Courtright, United States Volunteers, and an officer, whose
name escapes me, as Assistant Quartermaster and
Commissary,—numbering, in all, fourteen officers
and three hundred and twenty-one enlisted men. In
addition to the command, Colonel Carson had in-
duced seventy-two friendly Indians (Utes and Apaches), by promising them all the plunder that they

might acquire, to join the expedition. These Utes and Apaches are known among frontiersmen as "Mountain Indians," in contradistinction to the "Plain Indians," and make their homes in the Rocky Mountains, to the north and west of the Mexican town of Don Fernando de Taos. As Carson had been their agent at one time, and they knowing him well, he had little difficulty in inducing them to join him on an expedition against their old enemies.

The troops mentioned above were stationed at different posts in the Territory of New Mexico, and they were ordered to rendezvous at Fort Bascom, a frontier post on the Canadian river near the boundary line of Texas, on the fourth of November. The Quartermaster had received his supplies in a train of twenty-seven wagons and an ambulance, and the morning of the sixth of November found the command ready to stretch out, the horses having all been well shod, and after some difficulty in crossing the Canadian river, to the north side, the expedition was well on the war path before noon, and went into camp that night at the mouth of Ute creek, near the boundary line of New Mexico and Texas. From this

time the command moved on from day to day, with
only such incidents as usually accompany such expeditions, except that it was a new country to most of
us, as our campaigning had never extended to the
plains before this time, we heretofore having ope-
rated against the Navajoe and Apache Indians in the
immediate vicinity of the Rio Grande, extending
our scouting at times into the eastern and northern
parts of Arizona.   On our third or fourth day out
from Fort Bascom, we passed the vicinity where Kit
Carson had, fifteen or twenty years before this time,
pursued a marauding band of Comanches, who had
attacked a wagon train near Fort Union in New Mexico ; all the men of the train had been killed, including a Mr. White, an American, whose wife and child
had been taken prisoners.   Carson, who was in that
vicinity at the time, organized a party and proceeded
on the trail, and after several days, had come up to
them at this point.   They being well into their own
country had not anticipated being pursued so far.
The party of whites attacked them at early dawn,
drove them from their camp, and found only the
reeking bodies of Mrs. White and her child, still

warm, with their life's blood slowly ebbing away, the Indians having, as is usual with them, at the first sound of the attack, perforated the bodies of their prisoners with spears and arrows. Carson explained to us how their attack was made, the position of the Indian camp, where the bodies were found, etc., in his usual graphic manner.

The Indians with our command, on every night after making camp, being now on the war path, indulged in their war dance, which, although new to most of us, became almost intolerable, it being kept up each night until nearly daybreak, and until we became accustomed to their groans and howlings incident to the dance, it was impossible to sleep. Each morning of our march, two of our Indians would be sent ahead several hours before we started, who would return to camp at night and report. On the fifteenth we arrived and made camp at the Cañada de los Ruedes, or Wheel Gulch, so called from the fact that years before, when New Mexico was a State of old Mexico, the Mexican trains on their way to the States for goods, with their *carretas*, or ox carts, usually remained over here for repairs, and as the cottonwood trees were larger than at any other point on their route, they could obtain such a supply of new wheels as their necessities required — hence the name of " Cañada de los Ruedes."

We had up to this time followed on the old Mexican road from New Mexico, the first party that had passed over it for years, as it had been long in disuse, the usual route being by way of the Cimmaron and Arkansas rivers, several hundred miles farther north.   Near this point, the old wagon road left the valley of the Canadian, and turned abruptly to the north, while we, keeping to the right, found an old, unused Indian trail, which kept in the direction of the Canadian.   We had been fortunate in having good weather, for the season of the year, and something very unusual in scouting on the frontier, we had been successful in finding plenty of water, both for the men and for our animals.

On the afternoon of November twenty-fourth, after a short march of eighteen miles, we made camp at Mule Spring, having marched through the State of Texas and arrived in the western part of the Indian Territory.   Up to this time no indications of

hostile Indians had been observed, although Carson
made good use of his many years of frontier expe-
rience, by keeping his Indian scouts well out on
either flank. We had arrived at Mule Spring early
in the afternoon; had performed our usual camp
duties, and as the sun was about setting, many of
us being at supper, we were surprised to see our
Indians, who were lying around the camp, some
gambling, some sleeping, and others waiting for
something to eat from the soldiers' mess, spring to
their feet, as if one man, and gaze intently to the
eastward, talking in their own language quite excit-
edly. Upon questioning Colonel Carson, why this
tumult among our Indians, he informed us that the
two scouts that he had dispatched that morning, had
found the Comanches, and were now returning to
report the particulars. Although the returning
scouts were at least two miles distant, and, mounted
on their ponies, were hardly discernible, yet the
quick, sharp eye of our Indians made them out without difficulty. I must confess that I failed to see
them, until an Indian pointed out to me, away off on
the hill-side, two mere specks moving towards our

2

camp. And what was more remarkable, they had, by a single shout, in that rarefied, electrical atmosphere, conveyed the intelligence that they had found the enemy, and that work was to be done. But a short time elapsed before the two scouts arrived, and rode leisurely through camp, without answering any questions or giving any information, until they had found the Colonel, when they reported that they had, about ten miles in advance, found indications that a large body of Indians had moved that morning, with a very large herd of horses and cattle, and that we would have no difficulty in finding all the Indians that we desired. Carson immediately ordered all the cavalry, and the section of mountain howitzers, to be ready to move without delay. The Infantry, Company A, First California Infantry, under command of Colonel Abreú, was ordered to remain as escort to the wagon train, which was to stay in camp that night, and on the morrow was to move on and follow the trail of the command, until they overtook it.

Just before dark, Carson, with his command, moved out of camp, in light marching order, with strict orders that, during the night march, there should be no talking or smoking. Before twelve, we had descended again into the valley of the Canadian, which we had left four days before, and had also found in the dark, the deep-worn, fresh trail of thê hostile Indians. At this time, we believed that we were in the immediate vicinity of the enemy, and as nothing of their position was known to us, it was deemed prudent to remain where we were, and move on again just before daylight. This halt was very tedious. As I said before, no talking was allowed, (the few orders that were necessary, were given in a whisper,) lighting of pipes and smoking was prohibited; each officer and soldier upon halting, only dismounted, and remained holding his horse by the bridle rein until morning; and to add to our discomforts a heavy frost fell during the night.

As the first grey streaks of dawn appeared in the eastern skies, we mounted our horses, and proceeded on our new-found trail. Our order of march was, first on the right, Colonel Carson in company with the Utes and Apaches, who generally kept no regular order; next came about one-half of the cav-

alry force; then the section of mountain howitzers;
the balance of the cavalry bringing up the rear. We
had been moving but a few minutes, when I was informed that Carson wished to see me at the head of
the column. I urged my horse forward as quietly
as I could, and reported to him. As I did so, I re-
marked the funny appearance of his Indians, all of
whom were mounted in their own peculiar manner,
with their knees drawn up nearly at right angles,
and being cold, they were each of them enveloped in
their buffalo robes, standing high above their heads,
and fastened by a belt at their waist. Such a sight
was ludicrous in the extreme. Carson commenced
to say to me, in his own quaint way: "I had a
dream the night before, of being engaged with a
large number of Indians; your cannons were firing,"
—at this point of his recital, we heard a voice in
Spanish, on the opposite side of the river, cry out
"Bene-acá," "Bene-acá,"—"Come here," "Come
here." We knew that we had found a picket of the
enemy. Carson hastily ordered Major McCleave,
and B Company California Cavalry, with one of the
New Mexican detachments, to cross the river, as it

was easily forded. Our Indians, who had been riding leisurely along, at the first cry charged into a
clump of chapparel which was near by, and in a moment, as it seemed, came riding out again, completely divested of buffalo robes and all their clothing, with their bodies covered with war paint, and
war feathers in abundance, and giving a war-whoop
they dashed wildly into the river towards the enemy.
I was wondering at the wonderful transformation of
our Indians, entirely forgetful of the enemy, when
Carson gave orders for us to move down on our side
of the river, he being satisfied that the village would
be found within a short distance.

A few shots were fired on the opposite side of the
river, and we soon saw by the early morning light,
the enemy's picket, consisting of three mounted
Indians, rushing madly on, followed by the detachments that had been sent over. We had proceeded
but a short distance, when Carson ordered our force
to move on more rapidly, and strike the Indian village before they should become fully alarmed, while
he himself, with Lieutenant Heath's detachment,
remained as escort to the battery, the carriages of

which were so small that the cannoneers could not be
mounted, consequently they could not move as fast
as the rest of the command, which was composed
entirely of cavalry, it being remembered that the
infantry had remained behind the night before, at
Mule Creek, as escort to the wagon train. It was
not long before the cavalry had disappeared from our
sight, as we were now in the middle of the rich valley of the Canadian river, which was here about two
miles in width, with occasional clumps of cottonwood trees, and covered with tall dry grass, in many
places high above our heads when mounted on our
horses.   In fact, I remember that several times during that morning, when riding with Colonel Carson,
and keeping up a conversation, we could not see
each other, the tall dry grass intervening.   This tall
grass and an occasional clump of drift-wood, which
had been formed by previous freshets of the river,
made hard work for us to get along with the mountain howitzers.   The carriages having low wheels,
and tracking very narrow, the most constant care
and attention would not prevent their occasional cap-
sizing and consequent delay in righting up again.

We were an hour probably in getting through this wilderness, and getting out on to clear, hard, unobstructed earth again, by which time we could hear, far in advance, rifle shots thick and fast. The quick, sharp command, "Trot—MARCH," would be given to the battery, which would move out at a trot for a few hundred yards, when the dismounted cannoneers would soon be left stringing out a long way to the rear; "Walk—MARCH," would be resumed, so as to allow the men to regain their places, and after allowing them a short time to regain their breath, the same movements would be again and again performed.

At about nine o'clock, the firing in our advance, which was becoming more rapid, seemed to be moving forward faster than we were, or rather it seemed, that every minute, the distance between ourselves and the firing parties was becoming wider, yet we were all the time advancing. We now came upon a large number of cattle, belonging to the Kiowas, that were quietly browsing on the plain, entirely oblivious of war's destruction in their midst. Shortly after, we saw a number of our Indians, each having

his own separate herd of from twenty to fifty of the
enemy's ponies, and on getting them a short distance
away from each other, each would single out one of
the best of his respective herd, dismount, and plac-
ing his riding outfit upon his new steed, would leave
his own worn out pony to mark his individual property, expecting that the fight would be over in a few
minutes, when they were to return, and according
to their terms of contract for the campaign, each
would have his own separate herd of horses, which
he had collected, and which was marked by the horse
left by him.

A long low hill, running from the foothills across
the valley of the Canadian to the river, which was
here forced to the opposite side of the valley, next
met our view, over the top of which could be seen a
large number of what I supposed to be Sibley tents
from their shape and whiteness, and I so expressed
my opinion to Colonel Carson, who informed me
that they were Indian lodges made of buffalo hide,
whitened by a process practiced by all the Indians
on the plains.   I do not remember of having been
deceived at any time as I was by these lodges; posi-

tive I was that they were Sibley tents, and this opinion was also that of my enlisted men — buffalo lodges
are not used by the mountain Indians — but in the
next minute we passed through the centre of this village, when we were fully satisfied.

Our advance, which was a long way ahead of us,
had surprised the Kiowas in their lodges which
formed this village. The bucks or males had seized
their weapons and ammunition and retreated down
the river followed by our men, the women and children, before we came up, had also deserted the village and were hidden in the foothills on our left,
which we knew nothing of, unfortunately, as they
had an American woman and two children with them,
being the widow and children of a sergeant of Colorado volunteers who had been killed in the early part
of the season in western Kansas.

The firing continued in our front. Carson said to
me that we should proceed, and if the fight was not
over when we arrived it would soon be, when we
would all return and burn the lodges. At the same
time, he threw his heavy military overcoat on a bush
alongside the road, and advised me to do the same,

as we should return in a few minutes and get them
again. I did not do it, however. Some of my men
wished to take their overcoats and blankets from
the guns and leave them, but I would not allow them
to do so, and for once, my judgment was better than
Carson's, for he never saw that coat of his again,
while my own and those of my men did good service afterwards. But as we pushed on, the firing
seemed no nearer, until after we had made about
four miles from the village, when we saw our men,
dismounted and deployed as skirmishers, with their
horses corralled in an old, deserted, adobe building,
known by all frontiersmen as the Adobe Walls.
When we were within about a thousand yards of
this point, Carson, with Lieutenant Heath and his
detachment, put spurs to their horses and charged
forward to join in the fray. My men seemed to get
new life, and forgot all their fatigues, at the prospect of going into action, and but a few minutes
elapsed before we came into the centre of the field
at a gallop, and touching my cap to Carson, I received from him the following order: "Pettis,
throw a few shell into that crowd over thar." The

next moment, "Battery, halt! action right,—load with shell—LOAD!" was ordered.

It was now near ten o'clock in the morning, the sky was not obscured by a single cloud, and the sun was shining in all its brightness. Within a hundred yards of the corralled horses in the Adobe Walls, was a small symmetrical conical hill of twenty-five or thirty feet elevation, while in all directions extended a level plain. Carson, McCleave, and a few other officers, occupied the summit, when the battery arrived and took position nearly on the top. Our cavalry was dismounted and deployed as skirmishers in advance, lying in tall grass, and firing an occasional shot at the enemy. Our Indians, mounted and covered with paint and feathers, were charging backwards and forwards and shouting their war cry, and in their front were about two hundred Comanches and Kiowas, equipped as they themselves were, charging in the same manner, with their bodies thrown over the sides of their horses, at a full run, and shooting occasionally under their horses' necks, while the main body of the enemy, numbering twelve or fourteen hundred, with a dozen or more chiefs rid-

ing up and down their line haranguing them, seemed
to be preparing for a desperate charge on our forces.
Surgeon Courtright had prepared a corner of the
Adobe Walls for a hospital, and was busy, with his
assistants, in attending to the wants of half a dozen
or more wounded. Fortunately, the Adobe Walls
were high enough to protect all our horses from the
enemy's rifles, and afford ample protection to our
wounded. Within a mile of us, beyond the enemy,
in full and complete view, was a Comanche village
of over five hundred lodges, which, with the village
that we had captured, made about seven hundred
lodges, which allowing two fighting Indians to a
lodge, which is the rule on the frontier, would give
us fourteen hundred warriors in the field before us.

This was the prospect when the battery came on
the ground. A finer sight I never saw before, and
probably shall never see again. The Indians seemed
to be astonished when the pieces came up at a gallop
and were being unlimbered. The pieces were loaded
in a few seconds after the order was given, and were
sighted by the gunners, when the command "Number
one — FIRE !" was given, followed quickly by "Num-

ber two — FIRE !" At the first discharge, every one
of the enemy, those that were charging backwards
and forwards on their horses but a moment before
as well as those that were standing in line, rose high
in their stirrups and gazed, for a single moment,
with astonishment, then guiding their horses' heads
away from us, and giving one concerted, prolonged
yell, they started in a dead run for their village. In
fact when the fourth shot was fired there was not a
single enemy within the extreme range of the howitzers. Colonel Carson now assured us that the fighting was over, and that the enemy would not make
another stand, and gave orders that after a short halt,
to allow the men to eat something and to water our
horses, as neither man nor beast had received any
nourishment since supper time the day before, we
were to proceed and capture the Comanche village
before us. Accordingly the skirmishers were called
in, the cavalry horses were unsaddled, the artillery
horses unhitched from the pieces, and all taken a
hundred yards or more in our rear, to as fine a running brook of clear cold water as I ever saw on the
frontiers. The horses were allowed to drink their

3

fill, and then each one was picketed with a long lariat, or rope, to eat high, rich, uncropped grass. This accomplished, the officers and men proceeded to fish from the inmost recesses of their haversacks, such pieces of raw bacon and broken hard-bread as they had been fortunate enough to capture the night before on leaving the wagons. Each one had something to relate about the day's conflict, and each one was anxious to know what was to be the result of the day's operations.

Less than half an hour had elapsed, and Carson had not, as yet, given the order to saddle up, when the enemy were returning and seemed to be anxious to renew the conflict. Presently the order came to saddle up, the artillery horses were hitched in again, the cavalry horses returned to the inside of the Adobe Walls, the sharp, quick whiz of the Indians' rifle balls was again heard, the cavalrymen were deployed as before, and the fight was going on again in earnest.

During this fight, which lasted all the afternoon, the howitzers were fired but a few times, as the enemy were shrewd enough to know that their policy was to act singly and avoid getting into masses, although the detachments were kept on the field in the most exposed situations. At one of the discharges, the shell passed directly through the body of a horse on which was a Comanche riding at a full run, and went some two or three hundred yards further on before it exploded. The horse, on being struck, went head-foremost to earth, throwing his rider, as it seemed, twenty feet into the air with his hands and feet sprawling in all directions, and as he struck the earth, apparently senseless, two other Indians who were near by, proceeded to him, one on each side, and throwing themselves over on the sides of their horses, seized each an arm and dragged him from the field between them, amid a shower of rifle balls from our skirmishers. This act of the Indians in removing their dead and helpless wounded from the field is always done, and more than a score of times were we eye-witnesses to this feat during the afternoon. General G. A. Custer, in his "Life on the Plains," says of this Indian custom, in giving an account of an Indian fight near Fort Wallace, in 1867 : "Those of the savages who were shot from their saddles were scarcely permitted to fall to the ground, before a score or more of their comrades dashed to their rescue, and bore their bodies beyond the possible reach of our men. This is in accordance with the Indian custom in battle. They will risk the lives of a dozen of their best warriors to prevent the body of any one of their number from falling into the white man's possession. The reason for this is the belief, which generally prevails among all the tribes, that if a warrior loses his scalp, he forfeits his hope of ever reaching the happy hunting ground."

But to return again to my story : Quite a number of the enemy acted as skirmishers, being dismounted and hid in the tall grass in our front, and made it hot for most of us by their excellent markmanship, while quite the larger part of them, mounted and covered with their war dresses, charged continually across our front, from right to left and *vice versa*, about two hundred yards from our line of skirmishers, yelling like demons, and firing from under the necks of their horses at intervals. About two hundred yards in rear of their line, all through the fighting at the Adobe Walls, was stationed one of the enemy who had a cavalry bugle, and during the entire day he would blow the opposite call that was used by the officer in our line of skirmishers. For instance, when our bugles sounded the "advance," he would blow "retreat"; and when ours sounded the "retreat," he would follow with the "advance"; ours would signal "halt"; he would follow suit. So he kept it up all the day, blowing as shrill and clearly as our very best buglers. Carson insisted that it was a white man, but I have never received any information to corroborate this opinion. All I know is, that he would answer our signals each time they were sounded, to the infinite merriment of our men, who would respond with shouts of laughter each time he sounded his horn.

The course of the river could be discerned east-wardly at least a dozen miles, and there were several of the enemy's villages in that direction. We could see them approaching all the afternoon, in parties of from five to fifty, and it was estimated that there were at least three thousand Indians opposed to us,—more than ten to one. During the

afternoon, parties of the enemy could be seen at a
distance of two or three miles on either side, going
to the village that we passed through in the morning,
and they succeeded in getting all the stock that they
had left, in securing such valuables as had been left
by them in their lodges, and they also secured their
women and children and carried them to places of
safety.

The safety of our own wagon train now began to
be considered, as there were only seventy-five men
left with it, and it was feared that it might be captured by the large number of Indians that had passed
to our rear.   The most of our officers were anxious
to press on and capture the village immediately in
our front, and Carson was at one time about to give
orders to that effect, when our Indians prevailed
upon him to return and completely destroy the village that we had already captured, and after finding
our supply train, replenishing our ammunition, and
leaving our wounded, we could come back again
and finish this village to our satisfaction.   After
some hesitation and against the wishes of most of his
officers, at about half-past three Carson gave orders

to bring out the cavalry horses, and formed a column
of fours,—the number four man of each set of fours
to lead the other three horses,—with the mountain howitzers to bring up the rear of the column.
The balance of the command was thrown out as skirmishers on the front, rear and on both flanks, and we
commenced our return march. The enemy was not
disposed to allow us to return without molestation,
and in a very few minutes was attacking us on every
side. By setting fire to the high, dry grass of the
river bottom they drove us to the foot-hills, and by
riding in rear of the fire as it came burning towards
us, they would occasionally get within a few yards
of the column ; being enveloped in the smoke, they
would deliver the fire of their rifles and get out of
harm's way before they could be discovered by us.

During the morning's fight at the Adobe Walls, a
young Mexican boy, about eighteen or nineteen
years of age, belonging to one of the New Mexican
companies, was out on the line of skirmishers, and
as he was crawling forward, in reaching out his right
hand he placed it over the hole of a rattlesnake and
was bitten on the little finger. He passed near me,

as he came away from the line to find the Surgeon,
and as he was holding up his hand, I supposed that
he was wounded in that member, and said to him in
Spanish, "Que hay! que tienes?"—"Here you, what's
the matter?" He replied, "Un bibora!"—"Rattlesnake." He passed into the Adobe Walls, where
the Surgeon was located, who dressed his hand and
gave him a good stiff drink of whiskey. In a few
minutes he returned to the skirmish line, where he
remained until our return. His company was now
on our left flank, and after we had completed about
a mile of our return march, a Comanche rode up to
us in a cloud of smoke, when a sudden gust of wind
left him completely exposed within twenty feet of
the boy who had been bitten by the snake. They
both, at the same moment, brought their rifles to
their cheeks. The Indian fired a second before the
other, and missed his mark,—the boy immediately
returned the fire, hit his enemy in some vital part,
(he instantly fell from off his horse,) and rushed forward to secure his scalp. Some ten or fifteen of the
Comanches who were near, saw their friend fall and
rushed forward on their horses to secure the body

and bear it away out of our reach, as they had done a great many times during the day. The comrades of the Mexican soldier went to his assistance, kept the enemy at bay until he had finished the scalping operation, and then returned to their places in the skirmish line. This boy took the only scalp that our party secured during the whole day's fight. During this return march the howitzer in rear of the column succeeded in getting in a shell three several times on groups of the enemy.

Just before sundown we reached the village, which we found full of Indians trying to save their property from destruction. A couple of shells, followed by a charge of our men, drove them into the far end of it, when the work of destruction commenced, about half of the command being detailed to set fire to the lodges, while the rest of us were to keep the enemy in check. A small sand hill about twenty feet high was taken advantage of for the howitzers, and served as earthworks for the detachment. The pieces were loaded at the foot of the hill, and at the command of "By hand, to the front," they were pushed to the top, when the gunner would aim the piece, and at the command "ready" number four would insert the friction primer, and lying on his stomach, with no part of his body exposed, would wait for the command to fire. The piece on being fired would recoil, sometimes tumbling over and over and at others coming down fairly on the wheels to the bottom of the hill, when the other piece, having been loaded meanwhile, would be moved to the top and fired in its turn. The lodges were found to be full of plunder, including many hundreds of finely finished buffalo robes. Every man in the command took possession of one or more of these, while the balance were consumed in the lodges. There were found some white women's clothing, as well as articles of children's clothing, and several photographs; also a cavalry sergeant's hat, with letter and cross-sabres, cavalry sabre and belts, etc., being the accoutrements of the Colorado volunteer sergeant of which I have spoken before. We also burned an army ambulance and government wagon, with several sets of harnesses, which the Kiowas had retained from some wagon train they had captured during the previous summer.

I had forgotten to mention that with our seventy-two Utes and Apaches there were two old squaws, and the purpose for which they had accompanied the party had been a mystery to our men, but we ascertained now. It is well known to all frontiersmen that the mutilation of dead bodies (and they are often found mutilated so indecently that I cannot describe it here—a dozen times or more I have been eye-witness to this kind of mutilation myself,) is always the work of the squaws. When we passed the village in the morning, these two squaws were in these lodges, unknown to us, seeking for plunder. In the course of their search, they had found two old, decrepit, blind Kiowas and two cripples, who were unable to get out of their lodges when they were deserted by their people, and our two squaws soon placed them *hors-du-combat*, by cleaving their heads with axes. All four of these were found by our men when they were burning the village, the squaws themselves showing the men where they were, and claiming the merit of their slaughter.

The Comanches and Kiowas were driven from

lodge to lodge to the southern extremity of the village, and on reaching the last one, the party, num-
ing some thirty or forty, mounted their horses, and
at a run made from us towards the river, a twelve-
pounder shell, the last shot fired in the fight, explod-
ing in their midst, as a parting salute, just as the sun
was setting in the western horizon. The work of
destruction was soon finished,—every one of the one
hundred and seventy-six lodges, with their contents,
were consumed, together with the ambulance, wagon
and harnesses before mentioned.

It was some time after dark when the cavalrymen
had mounted their horses and had formed the column to return. The two gun carriages and the two
ammunition carts were loaded with the most severely
wounded, while the slightly wounded retained their
horses. The march now became the most unpleas-
ant part of the day's operations. The wounded were
suffering severely; the men and horses were completely worn out; the enemy might attack us at any
moment, unseen; and the uncertainty of the where-
abouts and condition of our wagon train, for you will
remember that we were now nearly two hundred and

fifty miles from the nearest habitation, or hopes of
supply, with the whole Comanche and Kiowa nations
at our heels,—all combined to make it anything but
a pleasant situation to be in. We had been moving
slowly on our return from the destroyed village
about three hours, when we saw away off on our
right several camp fires burning dimly, and approaching cautiously, we were soon welcomed by the chal-
lenge of a sentinel, in good, clear, ringing Saxon,
"Who comes there?" This was answered by our
men with cheers, for we were now assured that our
supply train was intact, and that starvation would be
averted for a season at least. But a few minutes
elapsed before we were in camp, the Surgeon made
the wounded as comfortable as possible, the horses
were unsaddled and unhitched from the pieces and
fastened to the picket line, a double guard was put
on, and then for blankets and sleep, hunger being
forgotten in our weariness.

This ended the day's work. The command had
been nearly thirty hours marching and fighting, with
an intermission of less than half an hour, and with
no other refreshment than that afforded by a single

4

hard-bread, and small piece of salt pork. The cas-
ualties of the day on our part were but two killed,
privates John O'Donnell and John Sullivan, of Company M, First California Cavalry, with twenty-one
wounded, two or three of whom died afterwards
from the effects of their wounds. One of our Utes
was killed and four wounded. The loss to the Comanches and Kiowas, was their village of one hundred and seventy-six lodges, buffalo robes, and all of
their winter's provisions, with nearly one hundred
killed, and between one hundred and one hundred
and fifty wounded.

Our wagon train had left camp at Mule Creek very
early in the morning, had followed our trail as well
as they could, and all day long had heard the howitzers each time they were fired. They knew that
we were engaged with the enemy, and the train was
kept in continuous motion, hoping to reach us before
the day closed; but night set in on them, and Colonel Abreú selected a good place for defence and
went into camp where we found them, they not having been molested by the Indians, although several
parties were seen by them during the day.

As the usual time for an Indian attack is just before daybreak, reveille was sounded at an early hour on the morning of the twenty-sixth, the command was distributed for an attack, but the sun soon rose upon us awaiting the onset. As none of the enemy were discovered, the officers and men, now that they had been refreshed by undisturbed slumber, bethought themselves of their stomachs, and I doubt if there was ever a heartier breakfast disposed of; all of the wild turkeys and antelope meat on hand were devoured,—calling upon the hunters to do their duty again. Our Indians were so tired the night before that they adjourned their "scalp dance," and sought the comfort of their buffalo robes; but, as we had been entertained every night until the fight by their "war dance," so for twenty-one days after, or as long as they remained with us, the monotony of the march was diversified by their own peculiar "scalp dance," and that with only one scalp, which they had purchased of the Mexican soldier whose exploit I have before mentioned.

We remained in camp during the day to allow the men and animals to recuperate, and never was needed

rest more welcome. The enemy did not seem disposed to molest us, but remained in full view, on an
eminence about two miles to the eastward of us.
The only incident of the day worthy of mention
was, that during the afternoon two of our Indians,
mounted, rode out leisurely on the plain towards the
Comanches; presently two of the enemy left their
party and rode towards us, when another party of
ten or a dozen left our camp, and then the same number left the camp of the enemy, like boys playing at
goal, and then another party from our camp, followed
by a like party from the enemy, until there were
over two hundred men of both sides moving at a
walk towards each other in the centre of the plain.
The leading parties of each side had approached each
other until only about two hundred yards of space
intervened, when shooting commenced, but before a
dozen shots had been exchanged the entire body of
the enemy turned their horses' heads towards their
camp, and left on a run, followed by our people for
a short distance, who afterwards returned to camp
unharmed.

Reveille was sounded early on the morning of the

twenty-seventh, and after breakfast orders were issued by Colonel Carson to saddle up, and commence the return march, much to the surprise and dissatisfaction of all the officers, who desired to go to the Comanche village that we had been in sight of on the day of the fight. It was learned afterwards that our Indians had advised Carson to return, and without consulting his officers the order was given and we commenced our return march.

We arrived at Fort Bascom on or about the twentieth of December without being molested by the enemy, where we remained a few days, when orders were received from the Department Commander for the different detachments to return to various posts in the Territory, and as the term of enlistment of the most of the men of my detachment had expired, I was ordered to Fort Union, where we arrived shortly after, on New Year's day, 1865.

General Orders, No. 4, Department of New Mexico, dated Headquarters, Santa Fé, N. M., February 18, 1865, which gives a detailed account of every operation with the Indians in that department for the entire year of 1864, says, on page 10, under date of November twenty-fifth : —

"Colonel Christopher Carson, First Cavalry, New Mexico
Volunteers, with a command consisting of fourteen commis-
sioned officers and three hundred and twenty-one enlisted men
and seventy-five Indians,— Apaches and Utes — attacked a Kiowa
village of about one hundred and fifty lodges, near the Adobe
Fort, on the Canadian river, in Texas; and, after a severe fight,
compelled the Indians to retreat, with a loss of sixty killed
and wounded. The village was then destroyed. The engage-
ment commenced at 8.30 A. M., and lasted without intermission
until sunset.

"In this fight, privates John O'Donnell and John Sullivan, of
Company M, First Cavalry, California Volunteers, were killed,
and Corporal N. Newman, privates Thomas Briggs, J. Jamison,
—— Mapes, Jaspar Vincent and J. Horsley, of Company B, and
—— Holygrapher, of Company G, First Cavalry, California Volunteers, Antonio Duro and Antonio Qauches, of Company M,
and H. Romero, of Company I, First Cavalry, New Mexico Volunteers, were wounded. Four Utes were wounded.

"Colonel Carson, in his report mentions the following officers
as deserving the highest praise: Major McCleave, Captain Fritz
and Lieutenant Heath, of the First Cavalry, California Volunteers; Captains Deus and Berney, First Cavalry, New Mexico
Volunteers; Lieutenant Pettis, First Infantry, California Volunteers; Lieutenant Edgar, First Cavalry, New Mexico Volunteers,
and Assistant Surgeon George T. Courtright, United States
Volunteers.

"The command destroyed one hundred and fifty lodges of the
best manufacture, a large amount of dried meats, berries, buffalo robes, powder, cooking utensils, etc., also, a buggy and

spring wagon, the property of 'Sierrito,' or 'Little Mountain,' the Kiowa Chief."

In 1867, about three years after the events narrated here, I was residing in a little Mexican village on the Rio Grande, Los Algodones, about forty-five miles south of Santa Fé, where I became acquainted with a couple of Mexicans who were trading with the Comanche and Kiowa Indians in the fall of 1864, and they informed me that they were at the Comanche village which we were in sight of, and that when the fight commenced they were held as prisoners and kept so for several days after we left that neighborhood; that in the village on the day of the fight there were seven white women and several white children, prisoners; they also informed me where the women and children of the village were hid when we passed through the Kiowa village on the morning of the fight, and that our enemy sustained a loss on that day, of nearly a hundred killed and between one hundred and one hundred and fifty wounded, making a difference with the official report, which guessed at thirty killed and thirty wounded. They also said that the Indians claimed that if the whites had not had with them the two "guns that shot twice," referring to the shells of the mountain howitzers, they would never have allowed a single white man to escape out of the valley of the Canadian, and I may say, with becoming modesty, that this was also the often expressed opinion of Colonel Carson.

PERSONAL NARRATIVES

OF THE

BATTLES OF THE REBELLION.

⸻✦⸻

A series of Papers which has been delivered before the Rhode Island Soldiers and Sailors Historical Society in Providence, and is being published under the general heading, " Personal Narratives of the Battles of the Rebellion." The following have already appeared :

No. 1.—THE FIRST CAMPAIGN OF THE SECOND RHODE ISLAND INFANTRY. By Elisha H. Rhodes. pp. 26. Price, 35 cents.

No. 2.—THE RHODE ISLAND ARTILLERY AT THE FIRST BATTLE OF BULL RUN. By J. Albert Monroe. pp. 31. Price, 35 cents.

No. 3.—REMINISCENCES OF SERVICE IN THE FIRST RHODE ISLAND CAVALRY. By George N. Bliss. pp. 32. Price, 35 cents.

No. 4.—MY FIRST CRUISE AT SEA AND THE LOSS OF THE IRON-CLAD MONITOR. By Frank B. Butts. pp. 23. Price, 35 cents.

No. 5.—KIT CARSON'S FIGHT WITH THE COMANCHE AND KIOWA INDIANS. By George H. Pettis. pp. 44. Price, 40 cents.

The style of these papers is graphic, simple and unpretending, the narrators intend to present only such scenes as they were personally witnesses of. The editions have been limited to 250 copies each — small quarto — elegantly printed — uniformly for the purpose of binding.

SIDNEY S. RIDER,

Publisher,

Providence.

www.ingramcontent.com/pod-product-compliance
Lightning Source LLC
Chambersburg PA
CBHW021432090426
42739CB00009B/1455